Robert Munsch

Heather Kissock

www.av2books.com

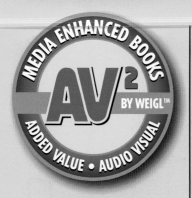

AV² provides enriched content that supplements and complements this book. Weigl's AV² books strive to create inspired learning and engage young minds in a total learning experience.

Your AV² Media Enhanced books come alive with...

Audio
Listen to sections of the book read aloud.

Key Words
Study vocabulary, and complete a matching word activity.

Video
Watch informative video clips.

Quizzes
Test your knowledge.

Embedded Weblinks
Gain additional information for research.

Slide Show
View images and captions, and prepare a presentation.

Try This!
Complete activities and hands-on experiments.

... and much, much more!

Go to **www.av2books.com**, and enter this book's unique code.

BOOK CODE

M 9 3 1 9 5 1

AV² by Weigl brings you media enhanced books that support active learning.

Published by AV² by Weigl
350 5th Avenue, 59th Floor
New York, NY 10118
USA
Website: www.weigl.com www.av2books.com

Library of Congress Cataloging-in-Publication Data

Kissock, Heather.
 Robert Munsch / Heather Kissock.
   p. cm. -- (Remarkable writers)
 Includes index.
 ISBN 978-1-61913-056-2 (hard cover : alk. paper) -- ISBN 978-1-61913-599-4 (soft cover : alk. paper) -- ISBN 978-1-61913-718-9 (ebook)
 1. Munsch, Robert N., 1945---Juvenile literature. 2. Authors, Canadian--20th century--Biography--Juvenile literature. 3. Children›s stories--Authorship--Juvenile literature. I. Title.
 PR9199.3.M818Z75 2013
 813'.54
 [B 23]

                    2012003164

Printed in the United States of America in North Mankato, Minnesota
1 2 3 4 5 6 7 8 9 0 16 15 14 13 12

062012
WEP170512

Senior Editor: Heather Kissock
Design: Terry Paulhus

Weigl acknowledges Getty Images as the primary photo supplier for this title.
Annick Press: pages 5 (Michael Martchenko), 13 (Sami Suomalainen), 18 (Sheila McGraw, Michael Martchenko), 19 (Michael Martchenko), 20, (Michael Martchenko), 21 (Michael Martchenko); Firefly Books: pages 13 (Sheila McGraw), 18 (Sheila McGraw); Scholastic Canada Ltd.: pages 20 (Michael Martchenko) 21 (Michael Martchenko).

Contents

Introducing Robert Munsch

To write children's books well, it is good to be a big kid yourself. Robert Munsch proves this every time he writes a book. This author is a kid at heart. As a result, he is one of the world's most successful children's authors.

Robert brings enthusiasm to everything he writes. His stories put children in weird and wacky situations. Angela flies an airplane in *Angela's Airplane*. Megan lets the pigs out of their pen in *Pigs*. Life is an adventure for the characters in his books and the people who read them.

Robert bases many of his stories on children he has met. He learns about their lives and what they do. He then tells their story to other children until he thinks the story is ready to publish. If you have a chance to meet Robert, perhaps he will write a book about you!

Robert Munsch is known for his exciting, animated personality.

Robert Munsch connects with children's hopes and fears in a way few people can. His characters are smart, brave, and independent thinkers. Robert's love for children and for storytelling are always present in his books, which have been **translated** into many languages and have sold more than 31 million copies worldwide.

✍ Robert Munsch uses silly faces and gestures to help his storytelling.

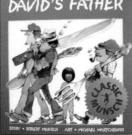

Writers are often inspired to record the stories of people who lead interesting lives. The story of another person's life is known as a biography. A biography can tell the story of any person, from authors such as Robert Munsch to inventors, presidents, and sports stars.

When writing a biography, authors must first collect information about their subject. This information may come from a book about the person's life, a news article about one of his or her accomplishments, or a review of his or her work. Libraries and the internet will have much of this information. Most biographers will also interview their subjects. Personal accounts provide a great deal of information and a unique point of view. When some basic details about the person's life have been collected, it is time to begin writing a biography.

As you read about Robert Munsch, you will be introduced to the important parts of a biography. Use these tips, and the examples provided, to learn how to write about an author or any other remarkable person.

Early Life

Robert Munsch was born on June 11, 1945, in Pittsburgh, Pennsylvania. His father was a lawyer, and the family lived in a large farmhouse just outside the city. The Munsch family was large. Robert was the fourth of nine children. He had five brothers and three sisters. Growing up in a large family provided Robert with the ability to understand different types of people. This would help him later in his writing career, as he created unique characters.

"I get a kid's name to use in the story and I still don't know what I am going to say. I just say whatever comes into my head and see if it's good. Usually it isn't. But sometimes it is very good. Lots of my books have started this way."
—*Robert Munsch*

Robert found school difficult. He was well-behaved in class, but he daydreamed often. He has said that the only reason he passed each grade was because no one wanted him to be in the same grade as his younger brother.

Pittsburgh is Pennsylvania's second largest city, after Philadelphia. Its population is more than 300,000.

Throughout his elementary school years, Robert wrote poems, which often were funny. No one, including Robert, paid much attention to the poems at the time. However, one person at school took special notice of Robert's interest in reading and writing. The school librarian, Sister Emma Jean, encouraged Robert to read books and even had him help her in the library. They worked together to **catalog** library books. Robert visited Sister Emma Jean often. Having Sister Emma Jean believe in him helped him feel good about himself.

Writing About Early Life

A person's early years have a strong influence on his or her future. Parents, teachers, and friends can have a large impact on how a person thinks, feels, and behaves. These effects are strong enough to last throughout childhood, and often a person's lifetime.

In order to write about a person's early life, biographers must find answers to the following questions.

1 Where and when was the person born?

2 What is known about the person's family and friends?

3 Did the person grow up in unusual circumstances?

School librarians help students find interesting books. Often, this leads to a lifetime love of reading.

STONY CREEK LIBRARY
1350 GREENFIELD PIKE
NOBLESVILLE, IN 46060

Growing Up

In high school, Robert continued to find it difficult to learn. His teachers believed he was an intelligent boy, but they were unable to help him improve his mathematics and writing skills. At the same time, Robert's moods often shifted from happy to sad. He found comfort in reading. Books became his friends.

"After all, while I made the best stories in the daycare centre, most of the other teachers made better playdoh."
—Robert Munsch

When Robert finished high school, he studied to become a **Jesuit** priest. While Robert was training to be a priest, he went to university. He graduated with a degree in history and then went on to earn a **master's degree** in **anthropology**.

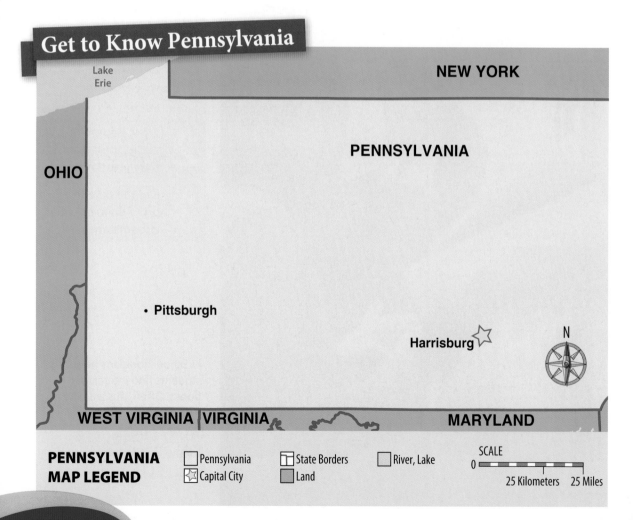

Get to Know Pennsylvania

Lake Erie

NEW YORK

PENNSYLVANIA

OHIO

• Pittsburgh

Harrisburg ☆

N

WEST VIRGINIA | VIRGINIA | MARYLAND

PENNSYLVANIA MAP LEGEND
☐ Pennsylvania   ⊓ State Borders   ☐ River, Lake
☆ Capital City   ▮ Land

SCALE
0 —————————
25 Kilometers   25 Miles

The Jesuits are active in the communities they serve, and Robert looked for ways to help others. Even though he was busy studying, Robert found time to work at a local **orphanage**. There, he discovered that he liked being around children and that they liked being around him.

Robert trained to be a priest for seven years. However, when he was 25, Robert was attacked by a mugger and left with serious injuries. He decided to leave the Jesuits for a year.

Robert's work at the orphanage led him to take a job in a daycare center. It was here that he met his future wife, Ann. Ann was working at the daycare while studying for a degree in child studies. They met while changing a child's diaper. Ann was touched by the way Robert handled children, and the two began dating.

✎ Many daycares act as preschools. Daycare workers plan various learning opportunities for the children who attend them.

Some people know what they want to achieve in life from a very young age. Others do not decide until much later. In any case, it is important for biographers to discuss when and how their subjects make these decisions. Using the information they collect, biographers try to answer the following questions about their subjects' paths in life.

1 Who had the most influence on the person?

2 Did he or she receive assistance from others?

3 Did the person have a positive attitude?

Developing Skills

Robert enjoyed working with young children and went back to university to learn more about them. During his studies, Robert became aware of his storytelling abilities. One day, while teaching at a preschool, he made up a story to tell the children. They loved it. This story later became one of his best-known books, *Mortimer*.

"Literacy is so important and it should be a family affair."
—*Robert Munsch*

Robert received his master's degree in child studies in 1973. He and Ann married that same year. They spent the early years of their marriage working in daycare centers in different parts of the United States. All the while, Robert practiced his storytelling skills with audiences of eager children. In 1975, he and Ann moved to the province of Ontario in Canada, so that Robert could take a job at a university. He taught students about caring for young children. He also ran a preschool. It was an ideal environment for Robert, and he added more stories to his ever-growing collection.

Robert still loves to tell stories to children. He often visits schools to read to students and make them laugh.

Robert's life was on a steady course. He had a happy marriage and a fulfilling job. However, his moods continued to swing. Ann suggested that Robert go to a doctor. The doctor found that Robert had **bipolar disorder**. The condition is treatable, and Robert's moods were brought under control with medication.

Robert was now ready to reach his full **potential**. Both adults and children enjoyed his storytelling. Many people urged Robert to write his stories down and try to get them published. At first, Robert ignored their comments. However, over time, he decided to give writing a try.

Writing About Developing Skills

Every remarkable person has skills and traits that make him or her noteworthy. Some people have natural talent, while others practice diligently. For most, it is a combination of the two. One of the most important things that a biographer can do is to tell the story of how their subject developed his or her talents.

1 What was the person's education?

2 What was the person's first job or work experience?

3 What obstacles did the person overcome?

Munsch worked at the University of Guelph in Guelph, Ontario. The university is best known for its science programs.

Timeline of Robert Munsch

1973

Robert earns a master's degree in child studies from Tufts University and marries Ann.

1945

Robert Munsch is born on June 11 in Pittsburgh, Pennsylvania.

1971

Continuing his education, Robert studies anthropology at Boston University, where he graduates with a master's degree.

1960s

After completing high school, Robert studies to become a Jesuit priest.

1969

Robert graduates from Fordham University with a Bachelor of Arts in history.

1975

Robert and Ann move to Canada, where Robert begins teaching at the University of Guelph.

1979

Robert's first book, *Mud Puddle*, is published.

1999

Robert Munsch is made a Member of the Order of Canada. This is a great honor for a Canadian citizen.

2009

Robert Munsch is honored with a star on Canada's Walk of Fame.

1986

Love You Forever, one of Robert's best-known books, is published.

1994

The New York Times lists *Love You Forever* as the best-selling children's book of all time.

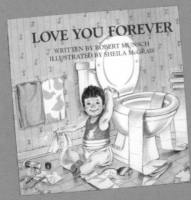

Early Achievements

Most authors start their writing careers by writing. They jot down their ideas and keep working on them until the words say exactly what the author means. Only when the author feels the story is at its best does it get made available for others to read.

"Most books I have written have been inspired by one particular child and its experience."
—*Robert Munsch*

Robert's writing career came only after he had been telling stories to children for more than 10 years. In a way, all of this storytelling was practice for Robert. He was learning how to write stories by telling them to the children who would be reading them in books. For this reason, he says, "I got it backwards!" At first, Robert just wanted to entertain the children who were in his care. He did this through storytelling. Years of storytelling provided Robert with the opportunity to find out what children liked and did not like in a story.

✍ Robert was 35 when he wrote his first book.

By watching the reactions of his audience, Robert was able to refine his stories after each telling. He would see what parts bored the children and what parts really interested them. He would then think of other ways to tell the story—what to take out, what to keep in, and what to change. Each time he told the story, it would change slightly. Robert would see how the children reacted to the revised story. If there were parts that still did not interest the children, he would make more changes and try telling it again. Sometimes, it was years before Robert was happy with the way children reacted to a story.

Robert believes that learning to write is similar to learning how to swim. People do not learn how to swim by reading about it. Likewise, a person will not learn how to write by reading a book that tells them how to write. In both cases, it is best to learn by doing it. "Practice makes perfect," and Robert believes that if people want to be writers, they should write as often as possible. Their writing skills will improve the more they practice.

Writing About Early Achievements

No two people take the same path to success. Some people work very hard for a long time before achieving their goals. Others may take advantage of a fortunate turn of events. Biographers must make special note of the traits and qualities that allow their subjects to succeed.

1 What was the person's most important early success?

2 What process does the person use in his or her work?

3 Which of the person's traits were most helpful in his or her work?

📖 Robert enjoys visiting schools and talking to children whenever possible.

Tricks of the Trade

Robert Munsch approaches the process of writing from an **oral perspective**. He thinks about how the story sounds when it is read out loud. Robert develops a story by talking instead of writing. To Robert, audience, **voice**, and revisions play important roles in story development.

Audience

Robert spends much of his time meeting the people who read his books. By talking to children, Robert can find out what they like to see or hear in a story. He learns what kinds of words they use when they talk. This helps him develop stories that interest children and use language that they understand.

Voice

To be a creative writer, an author has to have a unique way of presenting his or her story. Robert is known for using humor in his storytelling. He often uses words that some people do not think are proper, such as "peeing" and "underpants." These words help Robert reach his audience. This helps readers and listeners relate to the story he is telling.

Robert often gets ideas from the children he meets or letters they write to him.

Revisions

Robert's stories are rarely perfect when he first tells them. He often has to revise, or change, parts to get them just right. Robert bases the success of his stories on the reactions of his audience. If he is not getting the response he wants, he knows he has to rework the story until the characters, the plot, and the words all come together. Sometimes, it takes a long time for this to happen, but Robert feels it is worth the effort if the people reading and hearing his stories enjoy them.

"Even young writers can make their work better when they revise it."
—*Robert Munsch*

Robert likes to develop stories about the children he meets. He asks them if they want to volunteer to have a story made up about them. Once he gets a name, he starts creating a story right there. Sometimes, these stories become books.

Remarkable Books

All of Robert Munsch's books are popular. Children and parents seem to love everything he publishes. While most of Robert's stories sparkle with humor and spunky characters, they also show sensitivity to people's feelings and experiences.

Love You Forever

Before Robert and Ann **adopted** their three children, they had two babies that died. Robert wrote *Love You Forever* as a tribute to his children and the love that parents and children have for each other. The story follows the relationship of a mother and son. The relationship has happy and sad times as the boy grows up, but the mother's love remains constant. The son returns this love and passes it on to his own child later in life.

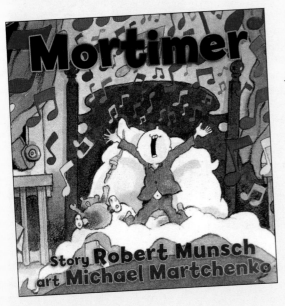

Mortimer

It is time for bed, but Mortimer does not want to sleep. He wants to sing! However, no one wants to hear him sing. They want him to go to sleep. Their attempts to get Mortimer to go to sleep lead to even more noise. Does Mortimer ever fall asleep?

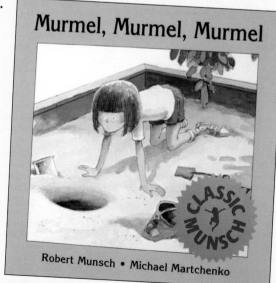

Thomas' Snowsuit

Thomas' mother buys him a new snowsuit for winter. Thomas thinks the snowsuit is UGLY, and he will not wear it. He refuses to wear it for his mother. He refuses to wear it for his teacher. He even refuses to wear it for the school principal. What makes him finally put it on?

Murmel, Murmel, Murmel

One day, Robin is playing in her backyard when she hears a funny sound coming from a hole in the ground. When she investigates, she finds a baby in the hole. Robin knows that she is too young to take care of a baby, so she tries to find someone who will. The story follows Robin as she meets potential parents.

David's Father

In this story, Julie makes friends with a boy named David. David seems like a nice boy, but Julie notices very strange things about the place where he lives. One day, David invites Julie into his house. Once inside, she learns that David's family is very different from her own. Julie discovers ways to embrace these differences.

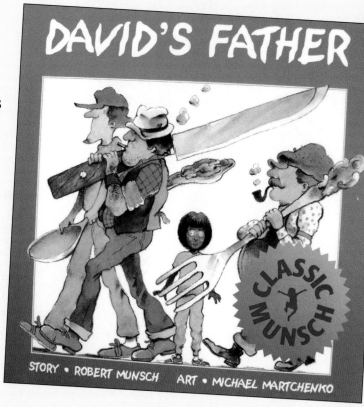

DAVID'S FATHER

STORY • ROBERT MUNSCH   ART • MICHAEL MARTCHENKO

CLASSIC MUNSCH

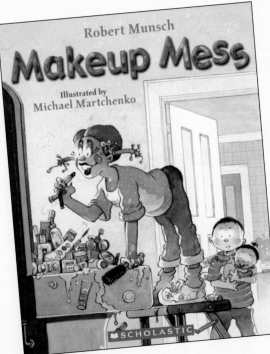

Robert Munsch

Makeup Mess

Illustrated by Michael Martchenko

SCHOLASTIC

Makeup Mess

Julie has saved up her money to buy makeup so that she can be pretty. She brings home the makeup and puts it on, but no one likes the way she looks. She decides to try again, but it does not look any better. People seem to think she looks better without the makeup, so Julie decides to stop wearing it. The problem is…she still has the makeup, and she spent her savings on it. Julie needs to get back her money, so she comes up with a plan.

Andrew's Loose Tooth

Andrew has a loose tooth that is not quite ready to come out of his mouth. It creates problems for Andrew whenever he wants to eat, and he wants it out of his mouth. His mom tries to get it out for him, but it will not come free. His dad tries to help, too, but with no luck. Other people try as well, but the tooth stays put. What can be done to help poor Andrew?

Something Good

When Tyya goes shopping with her dad, she decides to show him how to shop for "good" food and loads up the cart with cookies, sodas, chocolate bars, and ice cream. Tyya's dad gets mad at her, plants her in place, and tells her not to move. Unfortunately, a store clerk thinks she is a doll and tries to sell her. Tyya gets the last laugh, however, when her father tries to take her home.

From Big Ideas to Books

Robert's storytelling abilities became known throughout the university where he taught. One day, the wife of Robert's boss visited the daycare where Robert worked. She was a children's librarian, so she was very interested in learning more about Robert. She listened while he told the children some of his stories. Afterwards, she told Robert that he should write his stories down and try to get them published.

"I daydreamed all the time. I never paid attention. I never knew what was going on at school, or at home. I still don't know what's going on. I still daydream."
—*Robert Munsch*

Soon after her visit, Robert's boss began talking to Robert about getting his stories published. He gave Robert two months off from work to write. Robert waited until the end of the two months to begin writing. He quickly jotted down 10 of his stories and sent them to several publishing companies. He did not expect to receive any replies. One publisher responded favorably, and Robert's first book, *Mud Puddle*, was printed.

The Publishing Process

Publishing companies receive hundreds of **manuscripts** from authors each year. Only a few manuscripts become books. Publishers must be sure that a manuscript will sell many copies. As a result, publishers reject most of the manuscripts they receive. Once a manuscript has been accepted, it goes through

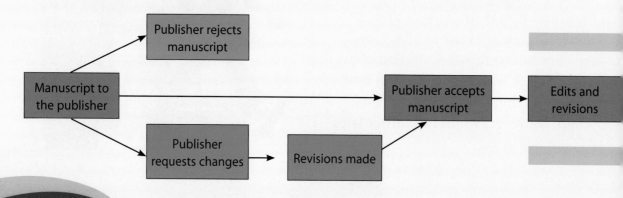

Mud Puddle was about a puddle that jumped on a boy. The book sold 3,000 copies in its first year. The publisher was happy with the sales and started publishing more of Robert's books. Over time, Robert's **reputation** as a talented writer grew, and his books became popular with children all over North America. Robert left his position at the university to write full time.

Robert sometimes enlists his family to help with his books. One of the stories Robert told children was a fairy tale about a princess who was rescued by a prince. When his wife heard the story, she told Robert that women today do not need men to rescue them. Robert changed the story so that the princess rescued the prince. This story later became a book called *The Paper Bag Princess*. Robert has also based a few of his books on his children's experiences.

✍ Robert believes that, if people want to be writers, they should write as often as possible. Their writing skills will improve the more they practice.

many stages before it is published. Often, authors change their work to follow an editor's suggestions. Once the book is published, some authors receive royalties. This is money based on book sales.

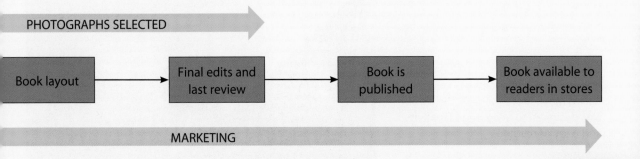

PHOTOGRAPHS SELECTED

Book layout → Final edits and last review → Book is published → Book available to readers in stores

MARKETING

Robert Munsch Today

Robert and Ann Munsch continue to live in Ontario, Canada. They adopted three children—two girls and a boy—in the early years of their marriage. Robert's children, Julie, Andrew, and Tyya, are now adults. Robert continues to write books and has more than 40 titles in print.

Robert and his books have been recognized in a variety of ways. An audiotape reading of *Murmel, Murmel, Murmel* won a Juno Award in 1985. A year later, *Thomas' Snowsuit* was awarded the Canadian Booksellers Association's Ruth Schwartz Award for best children's book. The Canadian Author's Association awarded Robert the Vicki Metcalf Award for Children's Literature in 1987. In 1992, the Canadian Booksellers Association named Robert the "Author of the Year."

The year 1999 was a very special year for Robert. He was awarded the Order of Canada. The Canadian government gives this honor to people who have had outstanding achievements in their field of work.

📖 In 2008, a museum exhibit based on Robert Munsch's books was launched. Called Much More Munsch, the exhibit was designed to encourage creativity and a joy of reading.

In August 2008, Robert suffered a **stroke**. This affected his ability to speak in normal sentences. Thankfully, he has recovered enough to tell stories to children. He had to stop writing for a while until he recovered.

In September 2009, Robert received a star on Canada's Walk of Fame in Toronto. In 2010, a public school was named for him. All the children at the Robert Munsch School signed a t-shirt and sent it to him. Robert still has many more stories to tell in the future.

Writing About the Person Today

The biography of any living person is an ongoing story. People have new ideas, start new projects, and deal with challenges. For their work to be meaningful, biographers must include up-to-date information about their subjects. Through research, biographers try to answer the following questions.

1 Has the person received awards or recognition for accomplishments?

2 What is the person's life's work?

3 How have the person's accomplishments served others?

Canada's Walk of Fame is located in Toronto, Ontario. It consists of a series of stars embedded along a series of sidewalks. Each star has the name of a famous Canadian.

Fan Information

Each year, classrooms of children write letters to Robert Munsch. They tell him how much they love his books and which ones are their favorites. Sometimes, they ask Robert questions about writing and tell him how much they would like to meet him. Robert loves to read his fan mail and to meet his fans. He sometimes decides to visit the people that have written him letters. Teachers and students have been surprised to find Robert at their school for a visit. Once the surprise is over, Robert quickly settles in to tell stories, answer questions, and, most importantly, meet his fans.

Munsch's website is full of information about his books and activities.

© 2012 Robert Munsch   Site by Barking Dog Studios

When Robert decides to visit a school or daycare, he often needs a place to stay. Instead of a hotel, he likes to stay with his fans and their families. **Raffles** are one way that the lucky family is chosen. While at their home, Robert spends as much time with the children as possible. They tell him their stories, and he tells them his. Robert gets new story ideas from many of these visits. Some of these children even get to be characters in his books.

Robert keeps in touch with fans through his website. Here, he posts information on his books, pictures from class and family visits, and artwork that some of his fans have sent him. People can even email Robert at the site.

Write a Biography

All of the parts of a biography work together to tell the story of a person's life. Find out how these elements combine by writing a biography. Begin by choosing a person whose story fascinates you. You will have to research the person's life by using library books and the reliable websites. You can also email the person or write him or her a letter. The person might agree to answer your questions directly.

Use a concept web, such as the one below, to guide you in writing the biography. Answer each of the questions listed using the information you have gathered. Each heading on the concept web will form an important part of the person's story.

Parts of a Biography

Early Life

Where and when was the person born?

What is known about the person's family and friends?

Did the person grow up in unusual circumstances?

Growing Up

Who had the most influence on the person?

Did he or she receive assistance from others?

Did the person have a positive attitude?

Developing Skills

What was the person's education?

What was the person's first job or work experience?

What obstacles did the person overcome?

Person Today

Has the person received awards or recognition for accomplishments?

What is the person's life's work?

How have the person's accomplishments served others?

Early Achievements

What was the person's most important early success?

What processes does this person use in his or her work?

Which of the person's traits were most helpful in his or her work?

Test Yourself

1 Where was Robert Munsch born?

2 Who was Robert's favorite author when he was growing up?

3 What did Robert plan to be when he graduated from high school?

4 Where did Robert and his wife meet?

5 How many children do Robert and his wife have?

6 Who convinced Robert to start writing?

7 What was Robert's first published book?

8 How many books has Robert written?

9 Which of Robert's books did the *New York Times* name the best-selling children's book of all time?

10 Where does Robert live?

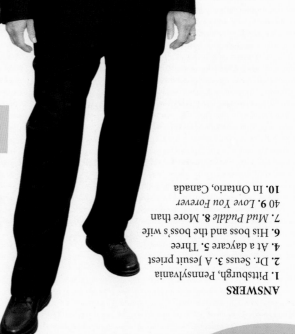

ANSWERS
1. Pittsburgh, Pennsylvania
2. Dr. Seuss 3. A Jesuit priest
4. At a daycare 5. Three
6. His boss and the boss's wife
7. *Mud Puddle* 8. More than
40 9. *Love You Forever*
10. In Ontario, Canada

Writing Terms

This glossary will introduce you to some of the main terms in the field of writing. Understanding these common writing terms will allow you to discuss your ideas about books and writing with others.

action: the moving events of a work of fiction

antagonist: the person in the story who opposes the main character

autobiography: a history of a person's life written by that person

biography: a written account of another person's life

character: a person in a story, poem, or play

climax: the most exciting moment or turning point in a story

episode: a short piece of action, or scene, in a story

fiction: stories about characters and events that are not real

foreshadow: hinting at something that is going to happen later in the book

imagery: a written description of a thing or idea that brings an image to mind

narrator: the speaker of the story who relates the events

nonfiction: writing that deals with real people and events

novel: published writing of considerable length that portrays characters within a story

plot: the order of events in a work of fiction

protagonist: the leading character of a story; often a likable character

resolution: the end of the story, when the conflict is settled

scene: a single episode in a story

setting: the place and time in which a work of fiction occurs

theme: an idea that runs throughout a work of fiction

Key Words

adopted: to raise someone else's child as one's own

anthropology: the study of human customs and cultures

bipolar disorder: a condition in which a person has extreme mood swings

catalog: to create a record of the books in a library

Jesuit: a member of a religious group that is part of the Roman Catholic Church

Juno Award: an award given to Canadian musicians and recording artists

manuscripts: drafts of a story before it is published

master's degree: recognition for completing a program of advanced learning at a university

oral: spoken

orphanage: a place for children who do not have parents

perspective: a way of regarding situations

potential: to further develop specific skills

raffles: ways of raising money that involve selling tickets for a prize

reputation: what is generally believed about a person's character

stroke: the sudden death of brain cells in a localized area due to inadequate blood flow

translated: put words into another language

voice: the way a person expresses his or her thoughts and ideas

Index

Log on to www.av2books.com

AV² by Weigl brings you media enhanced books that support active learning. Go to www.av2books.com, and enter the special code found on page 2 of this book. You will gain access to enriched and enhanced content that supplements and complements this book. Content includes video, audio, weblinks, quizzes, a slide show, and activities.

Audio
Listen to sections of the book read aloud.

Video
Watch informative video clips.

Embedded Weblinks
Gain additional information for research.

Try This!
Complete activities and hands-on experiments.

WHAT'S ONLINE?

Try This!	Embedded Weblinks	Video	EXTRA FEATURES
Complete an activity about your childhood.	Learn more about Robert Munsch's life.	Watch a video about Robert Munsch.	
Try this timeline activity.	Learn more about Robert Munsch's achievements.	Watch this interview with Robert Munsch.	**Audio** Listen to sections of the book read aloud.
See what you know about the publishing process.	Check out this site about Robert Munsch.		**Key Words** Study vocabulary, and complete a matching word activity.
Test your knowledge of writing terms.			**Slide Show** View images and captions and prepare a presentation
Write a biography.			**Quizzes** Test your knowledge.

AV² was built to bridge the gap between print and digital. We encourage you to tell us what you like and what you want to see in the future.

Sign up to be an AV² Ambassador at www.av2books.com/ambassador.